Letters

to a

Young Poet

Letters

to a

Young Poet

Rainer Maria Rilke

ISBN 978-1-60386-480-0

DIGITALIZED BY
WATCHMAKER PUBLISHING

Young Franz Xaver Kappus wrote to Rainer Maria Rilke in early 1903. To Kappus' delight, the poet replied. They continued a correspondence that lasted for nearly six years. The following are ten letters that Rilke wrote to Kappus, advising the young man on poetry and life.

Contents

Introduction

June 1929

It was late autumn of 1902—I was sitting under some ancient chestnuts in the park of the Military Academy in Wiener-Neustadt, reading. So deeply was I absorbed in my book, I scarcely noticed when the only civilian among our professors, the Academy's learned and kindly Parson Horacek, came to join me. He took the volume from my hand, contemplated the cover, and shook his head. "Poems of Rainer Maria Rilke?" he asked reflectively. He then turned the pages here and there, skimmed a couple of verses, gazed thoughtfully into the distance, and finally nodded. "So our pupil René Rilke has become a poet."

And I learned of the thin, pale boy, whom his parents had sent more than fifteen years ago to the Lower Military School at Sankt-Polten so that he might later become an officer. Horacek had been chaplain to that institution at the time, and he still remembered his former student perfectly. He described him as a quiet, serious, highly endowed boy, who liked to keep to himself, patiently endured the compulsions of boarding-school life and after his fourth year moved on with the others into the Military College, which was situated at Mahrisch-Weisskirchen. Here indeed it became apparent that his constitution could not stand the strain, for which reason his parents removed him from the school and let him continue his studies at home in Prague. How the course of his life had since shaped itself Horacek could not say.

After all this it is not hard to understand how I was determined in that very hour to send my poetic attempts to Rainer Maria Rilke and to ask him for his opinion. Not yet twenty, and close on the threshold of a profession which I felt to be entirely contrary to my inclinations, I hoped to find understanding, if in any one, in the poet who had written *Mir zur Feier.*[1] And without having intended to do so at all, I found myself writing a covering letter in which I unreservedly laid bare my heart as never before and never since to any second human being.

Many weeks passed before a reply came. The blue-sealed letter bore the postmark of Paris, weighed heavy in the hand, and showed on the envelope the same beautiful, clear, sure characters in which the text was set down from the first line to the last. With it began my regular correspondence with Rainer Maria Rilke which lasted until 1908 and then gradually petered out because life drove me off into those very

---

[1] 'Celebration of Myself'

regions from which the poet's warm, tender and touching concern had sought to keep me.

But that is not important. Only the ten letters are important that follow here, important for an understanding of the world in which Rainer Maria Rilke lived and worked, and important too for many growing and evolving spirits of today and tomorrow. And where a great and unique man speaks, small men should keep silence.

Franz Xaver Kappus
Berlin, June 1929

Letter One

Paris
February 17, 1903

Dear Sir,

Your letter arrived just a few days ago. I want to thank you for the great confidence you have placed in me. That is all I can do. I cannot discuss your verses; for any attempt at criticism would be foreign to me. Nothing touches a work of art so little as words of criticism: they always result in more or less fortunate misunderstandings. Things aren't all so tangible and sayable as people would usually have us believe; most experiences are unsayable, they happen in a space that no word has ever entered, and more unsayable than all other things are works of art, those mysterious existences, whose life endures beside our own small, transitory life.

With this note as a preface, may I just tell you that your verses have no style of their own, although they do have silent and hidden beginnings of something personal. I feel this most clearly in the last poem, "My Soul." There, something of your own is trying to become word and melody. And in the lovely poem "To Leopardi" a kind of kinship with that great, solitary figure does perhaps appear. Nevertheless, the poems are not yet anything in themselves, not yet anything independent, even the last one and the one to Leopardi. Your kind letter, which accompanied them, managed to make clear to me various faults that I felt in reading your verses, though I am not able to name them specifically.

You ask whether your verses are any good. You ask me. You have asked others before this. You send them to magazines. You compare them with other poems, and you are upset when certain editors reject your work. Now (since you have said you want my advice) I beg you to stop doing that sort of thing. You are looking outside, and that is what you should most avoid right now. No one can advise or help you - no one. There is only one thing you should do. Go into yourself. Find out the reason that commands you to write; see whether it has spread its roots into the very depths of your heart; confess to yourself whether you would have to die if you were forbidden to write. This most of all: ask yourself in the most silent hour of your night: must I write? Dig into yourself for a deep answer. And if this answer rings out in assent, if you meet this solemn question with a strong, simple "I must," then build your life in accordance with this necessity; your while life, even into its humblest and most indifferent hour, must become a sign and witness to this impulse. Then come close to Nature. Then, as if no one had ever tried before, try to say what you see and feel and love and lose. Don't write love poems; avoid those forms that are too facile and ordinary: they are the hardest to work with, and it takes great, fully ripened power to create something individual where good, even glorious, traditions exist in abundance. So rescue yourself from these general themes and write about what your everyday life offers you; describe your sorrows and desires, the thoughts that pass through your mind and your belief in some kind of beauty - describe all these with heartfelt, silent, humble sincerity and, when you express yourself, use the Things around you, the images from your dreams, and the objects that you remember. If your everyday life seems poor, don't blame it; blame yourself; admit to yourself that you are not enough of a poet to call forth its riches; because for the creator there is not poverty and no poor, indifferent place. And even if you found yourself in some prison, whose walls let in none of the world's sounds - wouldn't you still have your childhood, that jewel beyond all price, that treasure house of memories? Turn your attentions to it. Try to raise up the sunken feelings of this enormous past; your personality will grow stronger, your solitude will expand and become a place where you can live in the twilight, where the noise of other people passes by, far in the distance. - And if out of this turning-within, out of this immersion in your own world, poems come, then you will not think of asking anyone whether they are good or not. Nor will you try to interest magazines in these works: for you will see them as your dear natural possession, a piece of your life, a voice from it. A work of art is good if it has arisen out of necessity. That is the only way one can judge it. So, dear Sir, I can't give you any advice but this: to go into yourself and see how deep the place is from which your life flows; at its source you will find the answer to the question whether you must create. Accept that answer, just as it is given to you, without trying to interpret it. Perhaps you will discover that you are called to be an artist. Then take the destiny upon yourself, and bear it, its burden and its greatness, without ever asking what reward might come from outside. For the creator must be a world for himself and must find everything in himself and in Nature, to whom his whole life is devoted.

But after this descent into yourself and into your solitude, perhaps you will have to renounce becoming a poet (if, as I have said, one feels one could live without writing, then one shouldn't write at all). Nevertheless, even then, this self-searching that I as of you will not have been for nothing. Your life will still find its own paths from there, and that they may be good, rich, and wide is what I wish for you, more than I can say.

What else can I tell you? It seems to me that everything has its proper emphasis; and finally I want to add just one more bit of advice: to keep growing, silently and earnestly, through your while development; you couldn't disturb it any more violently than by looking outside and waiting for outside answers to questions that only your innermost feeling, in your quietest hour, can perhaps answer.

It was a pleasure for me to find in your letter the name of Professor Horacek; I have great reverence for that kind, learned man, and a gratitude that has lasted through the years. Will you please tell him how I feel; it is very good of him to still think of me, and I appreciate it.

The poems that you entrusted me with I am sending back to you. And I thank you once more for your questions and sincere trust, of which, by answering as honestly as I can, I have tried to make myself a little worthier than I, as a stranger, really am.

Yours very truly,
Rainer Maria Rilke

Letter Two

Viareggio, near Pisa (Italy)
April 5, 1903

You must pardon me, dear Sir, for waiting until today to gratefully remember your letter of February 24. I have been unwell all this time, not really sick, but oppressed by an influenza-like debility, which has made me incapable of doing anything. And finally, since it just didn't want to improve I came to this southern sea, whose beneficence helped me once before. But I am still not well, writing is difficult, and so you must accept these few lines instead of the letter I would have liked to send.

Of course, you must know that every letter of yours will always give me pleasure, and you must be indulgent with the answer, which will perhaps often leave you empty-handed; for ultimately, and precisely in the deepest and most important matters, we are unspeakably alone; and many things must happen, many things must go right, a whole constellation of events must be fulfilled, for one human being to successfully advise or help another.

Today I would like to tell you just two more things:

Irony: Don't let yourself be controlled by it, especially during uncreative moments. When you are fully creative, try to use it, as one more way to take hold of fife. Used purely, it too is pure, and one needn't be ashamed of it; but if you feel yourself becoming too familiar with it, if you are afraid of this growing familiarity, then turn to great and serious objects, in front of which it becomes small and helpless. Search into the depths of Things: there, irony never descends and when you arrive at the edge of greatness, find out whether this way of perceiving the world arises from a necessity of your being. For under the influence of serious Things it will either fall away from you (if it is something accidental), or else (if it is really innate and belongs to you) it will grow strong, and become a serious tool and take its place among the instruments which you can form your art with.

And the second thing I want to tell you today is this:

Of all my books, I find only a few indispensable, and two of them are always with me, wherever I am. They are here, by my side: the Bible, and the books of the great Danish poet Jens Peter Jacobsen. Do you know his works? It is easy to find them, since some have been published in Reclam's Universal Library, in a very good translation. Get the little volume of Six Stories by J. P. Jacobsen and his novel *Niels Lyhne,* and begin with the first story in the former, which is called "Mogens." A whole world will envelop you, the happiness, the abundance, .the inconceivable vastness of a world. Live for a while in these books, learn from them what you feel is worth learning, but most of all love them. This love will be returned to you thousands upon thousands of times, whatever your life may become - it will, I am sure, go through the whole fabric of your being, as one of the most important threads among all the threads of your experiences, disappointments, and joys.

If I were to say who has given me the greatest experience of the essence of creativity, its depths and eternity, there are just two names would mention: Jacobsen, that great, great poet, and Auguste Rodin, the sculptor, who is without peer among all artists who are alive today.

And all success upon your path!

Yours,
Rainer Maria Rilke

Letter Three

Viareggio, near Pisa (Italy)
April 23, 1903

You gave me much pleasure, dear Sir, with your Easter letter; for it brought much good news of you, and the way you spoke about Jacobsen's great and beloved art showed me that I was not wrong to guide your life and its many questions to this abundance.

Now Niels Lyhne will open to you, a book of splendors and depths; the more often one reads it, the more everything seems to be contained within it, from life's most imperceptible fragrances to the full, enormous taste of its heaviest fruits. In it there is nothing that does not seem to have been understood, held, lived, and known in memory's wavering echo; no experience has been too unimportant, and the smallest event unfolds like a fate, and fate itself is like a wonderful, wide fabric in which every thread is guided by an infinitely tender hand and laid alongside another thread and is held and supported by a hundred others. You will experience the great happiness of reading this book for the first time, and will move through its numberless surprises as if you were in a new dream. But I can tell you that even later on one moves through these books, again and again, with the same astonishment and that they lose none of their wonderful power and relinquish, none of the overwhelming enchantment that they had the first time one read them.

One just comes to enjoy them more and more, becomes more and more grateful, and somehow better and simpler in one's vision, deeper in one's faith in life, happier and greater in the way one lives.

And later on, you will have to read the wonderful book of the fate and yearning of Marie Grubbe, and Jacobsen's letters and journals and fragments, and finally his verses which (even if they are just moderately well translated) live in infinite sound. (For this reason I would advise you to buy, when you can, the lovely Complete Edition of Jacobsen's works, which contains all of these. It is in three volumes, well translated, published by Eugen Diederichs in Leipzig, and costs, I think, only five or six marks per volume.)

In your opinion of "Roses should have been here..." (that work of such incomparable delicacy and form) you are of course quite, quite incontestably right, as against the man who wrote the introduction. But let me make this request right away: Read as little as possible of literary criticism - such things are either partisan opinions, which have become petrified and meaningless, hardened and empty of life, or else they are clever word-games, in which one view wins today, and tomorrow the opposite view. Works of art are of an infinite solitude, and no means of approach is so useless as criticism. Only love can touch and hold them and be fair to them. Always trust yourself and your own feeling, as opposed to argumentation, discussions, or introductions of that sort; if it turns out that you are wrong, then the natural growth of your inner life will eventually guide you to other insights. Allow your judgments their own silent, undisturbed development, which, like all progress, must come from deep within and cannot be forced or hastened. Everything is gestation and then birthing. To let each impression and each embryo of a feeling come to completion, entirely in itself, in the dark, in the unsayable, the unconscious, beyond the reach of one's own understanding, and with deep humility and patience to wait for the hour when a new clarity is born: this alone is what it means to live as an artist: in understanding as in creating.

In this there is no measuring with time, a year doesn't matter, and ten years are nothing. Being an artist means: not numbering and counting, but ripening like a tree, which doesn't force its sap, and stands confidently in the storms of spring, not afraid that afterward summer may not come. It does come. But it comes only to those who are patient, who are there as if eternity lay before them, so unconcernedly silent and vast. I learn it every day of my life, learn it with pain I am grateful for: patience is everything!

Richard Dehmel: My experience with his books (and also, incidentally, with the man, whom I know slightly) is that whenever I have discovered one of his beautiful pages, I am. always afraid that the next one will destroy the whole effect and change what is admirable into something unworthy. You have characterized him quite well with the phrase: "living and writing in heat." And in fact the artist's experience lies so unbelievably close to the sexual, to its pain and its pleasure, that the two phenomena are really just different forms of one and the same longing and bliss. And if instead of "heat" one could say "sex";- sex in the great, pure sense of the word, free of any sin attached to it by the Church, - then his art would be very great and infinitely important. His poetic power is great and as strong as a primal instinct; it has its own relentless rhythms in itself and explodes from him like a volcano.

But this power does not always seem completely straightforward and without pose. (But that is one of the most difficult tests for the creator: he must always remain unconscious, unaware of his best virtues, if he doesn't want to rob them of their candor and innocence!) And then, when, thundering through his being, it arrives at the sexual, it finds someone who is not so pure as it needs him to be. Instead of a completely ripe and pure world of sexuality, it finds a. world that is not human enough, that is only male, is heat, thunder, and restlessness, and burdened with the old prejudice and arrogance with which the male has always disfigured and burdened love. Because he loves only as a male, and not as a human being, there is something narrow in his sexual feeling, something that seems wild, malicious, time-bound, uneternal, which diminishes his art and makes it ambiguous and doubtful. It is not immaculate, it is marked by time and by passion, and little of it will endure. (But most art is like that!) Even so, one can deeply enjoy what is great in it, only one must not get lost in it and become a hanger-on of Dehmel's world, which is so infinitely afraid, filled with adultery and confusion, and is far from the real fates, which make one suffer more than these time-bound afflictions do, but also give one more opportunity for greatness and more courage for eternity.

Finally, as to my own books, I wish I could send you any of them that might give you pleasure. But I am very poor, and my books, as soon as they are published, no longer belong to me. I can't even afford them myself and, as I would so often like to, give them to those who would be kind to them.

So I am writing for you, on another slip of paper, the titles (and publishers) of my most recent books (the newest ones - all together I published perhaps 12 or 13), and must leave to you, dear Sir, to order one or two of them when you can.

I am glad that my books will be in your hands.

With best wishes,
Yours,
Rainer Maria Rilke

Letter Four

Worpswede, near Bremen
July 16, 1903

About ten days ago I left Paris, tired and quite sick, and traveled to this great northern plain, whose vastness and silence and sky ought to make me well again. But I arrived during a long period of rain; this is the first day it has begun to let up over the restlessly blowing landscape, and I am taking advantage of this moment of brightness to greet you, dear Sir.

My dear Mr. Kappus: I have left a letter from you unanswered for a long time; not because I had forgotten it - on the contrary: it is the kind that one reads again when one finds it among other letters, and I recognize you in it as if you were very near. It is your letter of May second, and I am sure you remember it. As I read it now, in the great silence of these distances, I am touched by your beautiful anxiety about life, even more than when I was in Paris, where everything echoes and fades away differently because of the excessive noise that makes Things tremble. Here, where I am surrounded by an enormous landscape, which the winds move across as they come from the seas, here I feel that there is no one anywhere who can answer for you those questions and feelings which, in their depths, have a life of their own; for even the most articulate people are unable to help, since what words point to is so very delicate, is almost unsayable. But even so, I think that you will not have to remain without a solution if you trust in Things that are like the ones my eyes are now resting upon. If you trust in Nature, in what is simple in Nature, in the small Things that hardly anyone sees and that can so suddenly become huge, immeasurable; if you have this love for what is humble and try very simply, as someone who serves, to win the confidence of what seems poor: then everything will become easier for you, more coherent and somehow more reconciling, not in your conscious mind perhaps, which stays behind, astonished, but in your innermost awareness, awakeness, and knowledge. You are so young, so much before all beginning, and I would like to beg you, dear Sir, as well as I can, to have patience with everything unresolved in your heart and to try to love the questions themselves as if they were locked rooms or books written in a very foreign language. Don't search for the answers, which could not be given to you now, because you would not be able to live them. And the point is, to live everything. Live the questions now. Perhaps then, someday far in the future, you will gradually, without even noticing it, live your way into the answer. Perhaps you do carry within you the possibility of creating and forming, as an especially blessed and pure way of living; train yourself for that but take whatever comes, with great trust, and as long as it comes out of your will, out of some need of your innermost self, then take it upon yourself, and don't hate anything. Sex is difficult; yes. But those tasks that have been entrusted to us are difficult; almost everything serious is difficult; and everything is serious. If you just recognize this and manage, out of yourself, out of your own talent and nature, out of your own experience and childhood and strength, to achieve a wholly individual relation to sex (one that is not influenced by convention and custom), then you will no longer have to be afraid of losing yourself and becoming unworthy of your dearest possession.

Bodily delight is a sensory experience, not any different from pure looking or the pure feeling with , which a beautiful fruit fills the tongue; it is a great, an infinite learning that is given to us, a knowledge of the world, the fullness and the splendor of all knowledge. And it is not our acceptance of it that is bad; what is bad is that most people misuse this learning and squander it and apply it as a stimulant on the tired places of their lives and as a distraction rather than as a way of gathering themselves for their highest moments. People have even made eating into something else: necessity on the one hand, excess on the other; have muddied the clarity of this need, and all the deep, simple needs in which life renews itself have become just as muddy. But the individual can make them clear for himself and live them clearly (not the individual who is dependent, but the solitary man). He can remember that all beauty in animals and plants is a silent, enduring form of love and yearning, and he can see the animal, as he sees plants, patiently and willingly uniting and multiplying and growing, not out of physical pleasure, not out of physical pain, but bowing to necessities that are greater than pleasure and pain, and more powerful than will and withstanding. If only human beings could more humbly receive this mystery which the world is filled with, even in its smallest Things, could bear it, endure it, more solemnly, feel how terribly heavy it is, instead of taking it lightly. If only they could be more reverent toward their own fruitfulness, which is essentially one, whether it is manifested as mental or physical; for mental creation too arises from the physical, is of one nature with it and only like a softer, more enraptured and more eternal repetition of bodily delight. "The thought of being a creator, of engendering, of shaping" is nothing without its continuous great confirmation and embodiment in the world, nothing without the thousand-fold assent from Things and animals - and our enjoyment of it is so indescribably beautiful and rich only because it is full of inherited memories of the engendering and birthing of millions. In one creative thought a thousand forgotten nights of love come to life again and fill it with majesty and exaltation. And those who come together in the nights and are entwined in rocking delight perform a solemn task and gather sweetness, depth, and strength for the song of some future poet, who will appear in order to say ecstasies that are unsayable. And they call forth the future; and even if they have made a mistake and embrace blindly, the future comes anyway, a new human being arises, and on the foundation of the accident that seems to be accomplished here, there awakens the law by which a strong, determined seed forces its way through to the egg cell that openly advances to meet it. Don't be confused by surfaces; in the depths everything becomes law. And those who live the mystery falsely and badly (and they are very many) lose it only for themselves and nevertheless pass it on like a sealed letter, without knowing it. And don't be puzzled by how many names there are and how complex each life seems. Perhaps above them all there is a great motherhood, in the form of a communal yearning. The beauty of the girl, a being who (as you so beautifully say) "has not yet achieved anything," is motherhood that has a presentiment of itself and begins to prepare, becomes anxious, yearns. And the mother's beauty is motherhood that serves, and in the old woman there is a great remembering. And in the man too there is motherhood, it seems to me, physical and mental; his engendering is also a kind of birthing, and it is birthing when he creates out of his innermost fullness. And perhaps the sexes are more akin than people think, and the great renewal of the world will perhaps consist in one phenomenon: that man and woman, freed from all mistaken feelings and aversions, will seek each other not a opposites but as brother and sister, as neighbors, and will unite as human beings, in order to bear in common, simply, earnestly, and patiently, the heavy sex that has been laid upon them.

But everything that may someday be possible for many people, the solitary man can now, already, prepare and build with his own hands, which make fewer mistakes. Therefore, dear Sir, love your solitude and try to sing out with the pain it causes you. For those who are near you are far away, you write, and this shows that the space around you is beginning to grow vast. And if what is near you is far away, then your vastness is already among the stars and is very great; be happy about your growth, in which of course you can't take anyone with you, and be gentle with those who stay behind; be confident and calm in front of them and don't torment them with your doubts and don't frighten them with your faith or joy, which they wouldn't be able to comprehend. Seek out some simple and true feeling of what you have in common with them, which doesn't necessarily have to alter when you yourself change again and again; when you see them, love life in a form that is not your own and be indulgent toward those who are growing old, who are afraid of the aloneness that you trust. Avoid providing material for the drama, that is always stretched tight between parent and children; it uses up much of the children's strength and wastes the love of the elders, which acts and warms even if it doesn't comprehend Don't ask for any advice from them and don't expect any understanding; but believe in a love that is being stored up for you like an inheritance, and have faith that in this love there is a strength and a blessing so large that you can travel as far as you wish without having to step outside it.

It is good that you will soon be entering a profession that will make you independent and will put you completely on your own, in every sense. Wait patiently to see whether your innermost life feels hemmed in by the form this profession imposes. I myself consider it a very difficult and very exacting one, since it is burdened with enormous conventions and leaves very little room for a personal interpretation of its duties. But your solitude will be a support and a home for you, even in the midst of very unfamiliar circumstances, and from it you will find all your paths. All my good wishes are ready to accompany you, and my faith is with you.

Yours,
Rainer Maria Rilke

Letter Five

Rome
October 29, 1903

Dear Sir,

I received your letter of August 29 in Florence, and it has taken me this long - two months - to answer. Please forgive this tardiness, but I don't like to write letters while I am traveling because for letter-writing I need more than the most necessary tools: some silence and solitude and a not too unfamiliar hour.

We arrived in Rome about six weeks ago, at a time when it was still the empty, the hot, the notoriously feverish Rome, and this circumstance, along with other practical difficulties in finding a place to live, helped make the restlessness around us seem as if it would never end, and the unfamiliarity lay upon us with the weight of homelessness. In addition, Rome (if one has not yet become acquainted with it) makes one feel stifled with sadness for the first few days: through the gloomy and lifeless museum atmosphere that it exhales, through the abundance of its pasts, which are brought forth and laboriously held up (pasts on which a tiny present subsists), through the terrible overvaluing, sustained by scholars and philologists and imitated by the ordinary tourist in Italy, of all these disfigured and decaying Things, which, after all, are essentially nothing more than accidental remains from another time and from a life that is not and should not be ours. Finally, after weeks of daily resistance, one finds oneself somewhat composed again, even though still a bit confused, and one says to oneself: No, there is not more beauty here than in other places, and all these objects, which have been marveled at by generation after generation, mended and restored by the hands of workmen, mean nothing, are nothing, and have no heart and no value; - but there is much beauty here, because every where there is much beauty. Waters infinitely full of life move along the ancient aqueducts into the great city and dance in the many city squares over white basins of stone and spread out in large, spacious pools and murmur by day and lift up their murmuring to the night, which is vast here and starry and soft with winds. And there are gardens here, unforgettable boulevards, and stair cases designed by Michelangelo, staircases constructed on the pattern of downward-gliding waters and, as they descend, widely giving birth to step out of step as if it were wave out of wave. Through such impressions one gathers oneself, wins oneself back from the exacting multiplicity, which speaks and chatters there (and how talkative it is!), and one slowly learns to recognize the very few Things in which something eternal endures that one can love and something solitary that one can gently take part in.

I am still living in the city, on the Capitol, not far from the most beautiful equestrian statue that has come down to us from Roman art - the statue of Marcus Aurelius; but in a few weeks I will move into a quiet, simple room, an old summerhouse, which lies lost deep in a large park, hidden from the city, from its noises and incidents. There I will live all winter and enjoy the great silence, from which I expect the gift of happy, work-filled hours...

From there, where I will be more at home, I will write you a longer letter, in which I will say something more about what you wrote me. Today I just need to tell you (and perhaps I am wrong not to have done this sooner) that the book you sent me (you said in your letter that it contained some works of yours) hasn't arrived. Was it sent back to you, perhaps from Worpswede? (They will not forward packages to foreign countries.) This is the most hopeful possibility, and I would be glad to have it confirmed. I do hope that the package hasn't been lost - unfortunately, the Italian mail service being what it is, that would not be anything unusual.

I would have been glad to have this book (as I am to have anything that comes from you); and any poems that have arisen in the meantime I will always (if you entrust them to me) read and read again and experience as well and as sincerely as I can. With greetings and good wishes,

Yours,
Rainer Maria Rilke

Letter Six

Rome
December 23, 1903

My dear Mr. Kappus,

I don't want you to be without a greeting from me when Christmas comes and when you, in the midst of the holiday, are bearing your solitude more heavily than usual. But when you notice that it is vast, you should be happy; for what (you should ask yourself) would a solitude be that was not vast; there is only one solitude, and it is vast, heavy, difficult to bear, and almost everyone has hours when he would gladly exchange it for any kind of sociability, however trivial or cheap, for the tiniest outward agreement with the first person who comes along, the most unworthy... But perhaps these are the very hours during which solitude grows; for its growing is painful as the growing of boys and sad as the beginning of spring. But that must not confuse you. What is necessary, after all, is only this: solitude, vast inner solitude. To walk inside yourself and meet no one for hours - that is what you must be able to attain. To be solitary as you were when you were a child, when the grownups walked around involved with matters that seemed large and important because they looked so busy and because you didn't understand a thing about what they were doing.

And when you realize that their activities are shabby, that their vocations are petrified and no longer connected with life, why not then continue to look upon it all as a child would, as if you were looking at something unfamiliar, out of the depths of your own world, from the vastness of your own solitude, which is itself work and status and vocation? Why should you want to give up a child's wise not-understanding in exchange for defensiveness and scorn, since not understanding is, after all, a way of being alone, whereas defensiveness and scorn are a participation in precisely what, by these means, you want to separate yourself from.

Think, dear Sir, of the world that you carry inside you, and call this thinking whatever you want to: a remembering of your own childhood or a yearning toward a future of your own - only be attentive to what is arising within you, and place that above everything you perceive around you. What is happening in your innermost self is worthy of your entire love; somehow you must find a way to work at it, and not lose too much time or too much courage in clarifying your attitude toward people. Who says that you have any attitude at all? - I know, your profession is hard and full of things that contradict you, and I foresaw your lament and knew that it would come. Now that it has come, there is nothing I can say to reassure you, I can only suggest that perhaps all professions are like that, filled with demands, filled with hostility toward the individual, saturated as it were with the hatred of those who find themselves mute and sullen in an insipid duty. The situation you must live in now is not more heavily burdened with conventions, prejudices, and false ideas than all the other situations, and if there are some that pretend to offer a greater freedom, there is nevertheless none that is, in itself, vast and spacious and connected to the important Things that the truest kind of life consists of. Only the individual who is solitary is placed under the deepest laws like a Thing, and when he walks out into the rising dawn or looks out into the event-filled evening and when he feels what is happening there, all situations drop from him as if from a dead man, though he stands in the midst of pure life. What you, dear Mr. Kappus, now have to experience as an officer, you would have felt in just the same way in any of the established professions; yes, even if, outside any position, you had simply tried to find some easy and independent contact with society, this feeling of being hemmed in would not have been spared you. It is like this everywhere;

but that is no cause for anxiety or sadness; if there is nothing you can share with other people, try to be close to Things; they will not abandon you; and the nights are still there, and the winds that move through the trees and across many lands; everything in the world of Things and animals is still filled with happening, which you can take part in; and children are still the way you were as a child, sad and happy in just the same way - and if you think of your childhood, you once again live among them, among the solitary children, and the grownups are nothing, and their dignity has no value.

And if it frightens and torments you to think of childhood and of the simplicity and silence that accompanies it, because you can no longer believe in God, who appears in it everywhere, then ask yourself, dear Mr. Kappus, whether you have really lost God. Isn't it much truer to say that you have never yet possessed him? For when could that have been? Do you think that a child can hold him, him whom grown men bear only with great effort and whose weight crushes the old? Do you suppose that someone who really has him could lose him like a little stone? Or don't you think that someone who once had him could only be lost by him? But if you realize that he did not exist in your childhood, and did not exist previously, if you suspect that Christ was deluded by his yearning and Muhammad deceived by his pride - and if you are terrified to feel that even now he does not exist, even at this moment when we are talking about him - what justifies you then, if he never existed, in missing him like someone who has passed away and in searching for him as though he were lost?

Why don't you think of him as the one who is coming, who has been approaching from all eternity, the one who will someday arrive, the ultimate fruit of a tree whose leaves we are? What keeps you from projecting his birth into the ages that are coming into existence, and living your life as a painful and lovely day in the history of a great pregnancy? Don't you see how everything that happens is again and again a beginning, and couldn't it be His beginning, since, in itself, starting is always so beautiful? If he is the most perfect one, must not what is less perfect precede him, so that he can choose himself out of fullness and superabundance? - Must he not be the last one, so that he can include everything in himself, and what meaning would we have if he whom we are longing for has already existed?

As bees gather honey, so we collect what is sweetest out of all things and build Him. Even with the trivial, with the insignificant (as long as it is done out of love) we begin, with work and with the repose that comes afterward, with a silence or with a small solitary joy, with everything that we do alone, without anyone to join or help us, we start Him whom we will not live to see, just as our ancestors could not live to see us. And yet they, who passed away long ago, still exist in us, as predisposition, as burden upon our fate, as murmuring blood, and as gesture that rises up from the depths of time.

Is there anything that can deprive you of the hope that in this way you will someday exist in Him, who is the farthest, the outermost limit?

Dear Mr. Kappus, celebrate Christmas in this devout feeling, that perhaps He needs this very anguish of yours in order to begin; these very days of your transition are perhaps the time when everything in you is working at Him, as you once worked at Him in your childhood, breathlessly. Be patient and without bitterness, and realize that the least we can do is to make coming into existence no more difficult for Him than the earth does for spring when it wants to come.

And be glad and confident.

Yours,
Rainer Maria Rilke

Letter Seven

Rome
May 14, 1904

My dear Mr. Kappus,

Much time has passed since I received your last letter. Please don't hold that against me; first it was work, then a number of interruptions, and finally poor health that again and again kept me from answering, because I wanted my answer to come to you out of peaceful and happy days. Now I feel somewhat better again (the beginning of spring with its moody, bad-tempered transitions was hard to bear here too) and once again, dear Mr. Kappus, I can greet you and talk to you (which I do with real pleasure) about this and that in response to your letter, as well as I can.

You see: I have copied out your sonnet, because I found that it is lovely and simple and born in the shape that it moves in with such quiet decorum. It is the best poem of yours that you have let me read. And now I am giving you this copy because I know that it is important and full of new experience to rediscover a work of one's own in someone else's handwriting. Read the poem as if you had never seen it before, and you will feel in your innermost being how very much it is your own.

It was a pleasure for me to read this sonnet and your letter, often; I thank you for both.

And you should not let yourself be confused in your solitude by the fact that there is something in you that wants to move out of it. This very wish, if you use it calmly and prudently and like a tool, will help you spread out your solitude over a great distance. Most people have (with the help of conventions) turned their solutions toward what is easy and toward the easiest side of the easy; but it is clear that we must trust in what is difficult; everything alive trusts in it, everything, in Nature grows and defends itself any way it can and is spontaneously itself, tries to be itself at all costs and against all opposition. We know little, but that we must trust in what is difficult is a certainty that will never abandon us; it is good to be solitary, for solitude is difficult; that something is difficult must be one more reason for us to do it.

It is also good to love: because love is difficult. For one human being to love another human being: that is perhaps the most difficult task that has been entrusted to us, the ultimate task, the final test and proof, the work for which all other work is merely preparation. That is why young people, who are beginners in everything, are not yet capable of love: it is something they must learn. With their whole being, with all their forces, gathered around their solitary, anxious, upward-beating heart, they must learn to love. But learning-time is always a long, secluded time, and therefore loving, for a long time ahead and far on into life, is: solitude, a heightened and deepened kind of aloneness for the person who loves. Loving does not at first mean merging, surrendering, and uniting with another person (for what would a union be of two people who are unclarified, unfinished, and still incoherent?), it is a high inducement for the individual to ripen, to become something in himself, to become world, to become world in himself for the sake of another person; it is a great, demanding claim on him, something that chooses him and calls him to vast distances. Only in this sense, as the task of working on themselves ("to hearken and to hammer day and night"), may young people use the love that is given to them. Merging and surrendering and every kind of communion is not for them (who must still, for a long, long time, save and gather themselves); it is the ultimate, is perhaps that for which human lives are as yet barely large enough.

But this is what young people are so often and so disastrously wrong in doing: they (who by their very nature are impatient) fling themselves at each other when love takes hold of them, they scatter themselves, just as they are, in all their messiness, disorder, bewilderment... And what can happen then? What can life do with this heap of half-broken things that they call their communion and that they would like to call their happiness, if that were possible, and their future? And so each of them loses himself for the sake of the other person, and loses the other, and many others who still wanted to come. And loses the vast distances and possibilities, gives up the approaching and fleeing of gentle, prescient Things in exchange for an unfruitful confusion, out of which nothing more can come; nothing but a bit of disgust, disappointment, and poverty, and the escape into one of the many conventions that have been put up in great numbers like public shelters on this most dangerous road. No area of human experience is so extensively provided with conventions as this one is: there are life-preservers of the most varied invention, boats and water wings; society has been able to create refuges of every sort, for since it preferred to take love life as an amusement, it also had to give it an easy form, cheap, safe, and sure, as public amusements are.

It is true that many young people who love falsely, i.e., simply surrendering themselves and giving up their solitude (the average person will of course always go on doing that), feel oppressed by their failure and want to make the situation they have landed in livable and fruitful in their own, personal way. For their nature tells them that the questions of love, even more than everything else that is important, cannot be resolved publicly and according to this or that agreement; that they are questions, intimate questions from one human being to another, which in any case require a new, special, wholly personal answer. But how can they, who have already flung themselves together and can no longer tell whose outlines are whose, who thus no longer possess anything of their own, how can they find a way out of themselves, out of the depths of their already buried solitude?

They act out of mutual helplessness, and then if, with the best of intentions, they try to escape the convention that is approaching them (marriage, for example), they fall into the clutches of some less obvious but just as deadly conventional solution. For then everything around them is convention. Wherever people act out of a prematurely fused, muddy communion, every action is conventional: every relation that such confusion leads to has its own convention, however unusual (i.e., in the ordinary sense immoral) it may be; even separating would be a conventional step, an impersonal, accidental decision without strength and without fruit.

Whoever looks seriously will find that neither for death, which is difficult, nor for difficult love has any clarification, any solution, any hint of a path been perceived; and for both these tasks, which we carry wrapped up and hand, on without opening, there is no general, agreed-upon rule that can be discovered. But in the same measure in which we begin to test life as individuals, these great Things will come to meet us, the individuals, with greater intimacy. The claims that the difficult work of love makes upon our development are greater than life, and we, as beginners, are not equal to them. But if we nevertheless endure and take this love upon us as burden and apprenticeship, instead of losing ourselves in the whole easy and frivolous game behind which people have hidden from the most solemn solemnity of their being, then a small advance and a lightening will perhaps be perceptible to those who come long after us. That would be much.

We are only just now beginning to consider the relation of one individual to a second individual objectively and without prejudice, and our attempts to live such relationships have no model before them. And yet in the changes that time has brought about there are already many things that can help our timid novitiate.

The girl and the woman, in their new, individual unfolding, will only in passing be imitators of male behavior and misbehavior and repeaters of male professions. After the uncertainty of such transitions, it will become obvious that women were going through the abundance and variation of those (often ridiculous) disguises just so that they could purify their own essential nature and wash out the deforming influences of the other sex. Women, in whom life lingers and dwells more immediately , more fruitfully, and more confidently, must surely have become riper and more human in their depths than light, easygoing man, who is not pulled down beneath the surface of life by the weight of any bodily fruit and who, arrogant and hasty, undervalues what he thinks he loves. This humanity of woman, carried in her womb through all her suffering and humiliation, will come to light when she has stripped off the conventions of mere femaleness in the transformations of her outward status, and those men who do not yet feel it approaching will be astonished by it. Someday (and even now, especially in the countries of northern Europe, trustworthy signs are already speaking and shining), someday there will be girls and women whose name will no longer mean the mere opposite of the male, but something in itself, something that makes one think not of any complement and limit, but only of life and reality: the female human being.

This advance (at first very much against the will of the outdistanced men) will transform the love experience, which is now filled with error, will change it from the ground up, and reshape it into a relationship that is meant to be between one human being and another, no longer one that flows from man to woman. And this more human love (which will fulfill itself with infinite consideration and gentleness, and kindness and clarity in binding and releasing) will resemble what we are now preparing painfully and with great struggle: the love that consists in this: that two solitudes protect and border and greet each other.

And one more thing: Don't think that the great love which was once granted to you, when you were a boy, has been lost; how can you know whether vast and generous wishes didn't ripen in you at that time, and purposes by which you are still living today? I believe that that love remains so strong and intense in your memory because it was your first deep aloneness and the first inner work that you did on your life. - All good wishes to you, dear Mr. Kappus!

Yours,
Rainer Maria Rilke

Letter Eight

Borgeby gard, Fladie, Sweden
August 12, 1904

I want to talk to you again for a little while, dear Mr. Kappus, although there is almost nothing I can say that will help you, and I can hardly find one useful word. You have had many sadnesses, large ones, which passed. And you say that even this passing was difficult and upsetting for you. But please, ask yourself whether these large sadnesses haven't rather gone right through you. Perhaps many things inside you have been transformed; perhaps somewhere, someplace deep inside your being, you have undergone important changes while you were sad. The only sadnesses that are dangerous and unhealthy are the ones that we carry around in public in order to drown them out with the noise; like diseases that are treated superficially and foolishly, they just withdraw and after a short interval break out again all the more terribly; and gather inside us and are life, are life that is unlived, rejected, lost, life that we can die of.

If only it were possible for us to see farther than our knowledge reaches, and even a little beyond the outworks of our presentiment, perhaps we would bear our sadnesses with greater trust than we have in our joys. For they are the moments when something new has entered us, something unknown; our feelings grow mute in shy embarrassment, everything in us withdraws, a silence arises, and the new experience, which no one knows, stands in the midst of it all and says nothing.

It seems to me that almost all our sadnesses are moments of tension, which we feel as paralysis because we no longer hear our astonished emotions living. Because we are alone with the unfamiliar presence that has entered us; because everything we trust and are used to is for a moment taken away from us; because we stand in the midst of a transition where we cannot remain standing. That is why the sadness passes: the new presence inside us, the presence that has been added, has entered our heart, has gone into its innermost chamber and is no longer even there, is already in our bloodstream. And we don't know what it was. We could easily be made to believe that nothing happened, and yet we have changed, as a house that a guest has entered changes. We can't say who has come, perhaps we will never know, but many signs indicate that the future enters us in this way in order to be transformed in us, long before it happens. And that is why it is so important to be solitary and attentive when one is sad: because the seemingly uneventful and motionless moment when our future steps into us is so much closer to life than that other loud and accidental point of time when it happens to us as if from outside. The quieter we are, the more patient and open we are in our sadnesses, the more deeply and serenely the new presence can enter us, and the more we can make it our own, the more it becomes our fate; and later on, when it "happens" (that is, steps forth out of us to other people), we will feel related and close to it in our innermost being. And that is necessary. It is necessary - and toward this point our development will move, little by little - that nothing alien happen to us, but only what has long been our own. People have already had to rethink so many concepts of motion; and they will also gradually come to realize that what we call fate does not come into us from the outside, but emerges from us. It is only because so many people have not absorbed and transformed their fates while they were living in them that they have not realized what was emerging from them; it was so alien to them that, in their confusion and fear, they thought it must have entered them at the very moment they became aware of it, for they swore they had never before found anything like that inside them. just as people for a long time had a wrong idea about the sun's motion, they are even now wrong about the motion of what is to come. The future stands still, dear Mr. Kappus, but we move in infinite space.

How could it not be difficult for us?

And to speak of solitude again, it becomes clearer and clearer that fundamentally this is nothing that one can choose or refrain from. We are solitary. We can delude ourselves about this and act as if it were not true. That is all. But how much better it is to recognize that we are alone; yes, even to begin from this realization. It will, of course, make us dizzy; for all points that our eyes used to rest on are taken away from us, there is no longer anything near us, and everything far away is infinitely far. A man taken out of his room and, almost without preparation or transition, placed on the heights of a great mountain range, would feel something like that: an unequalled insecurity, an abandonment to the nameless, would almost annihilate him. He would feel he was falling or think he was being catapulted out into space or exploded into a thousand pieces: what a colossal lie his brain would have to invent in order to catch up with and explain the situation of his senses. That is how all distances, all measures, change for the person who becomes solitary; many of these changes occur suddenly and then, as with the man on the mountaintop, unusual fantasies and strange feelings arise, which seem to grow out beyond all that is bearable. But it is necessary for us to experience that too. We must accept our reality as vastly as we possibly can; everything, even the unprecedented, must be possible within it. This is in the end the only kind of courage that is required of us: the courage to face the strangest, most unusual, most inexplicable experiences that can meet us. The fact that people have in this sense been cowardly has done infinite harm to life; the experiences that are called it apparitions, the whole so-called "spirit world," death, all these Things that are so closely related to us, have through our daily defensiveness been so entirely pushed out of life that the senses with which we might have been able to grasp them have atrophied. To say nothing of God. But the fear of the inexplicable has not only impoverished the reality of the individual; it has also narrowed the relationship between one human being and another, which has as it were been lifted out of the riverbed of infinite possibilities and set down in a fallow place on the bank, where nothing happens. For it is not only indolence that causes human relationships to be repeated from case to case with such unspeakable monotony and boredom; it is timidity before any new, inconceivable experience, which we don't think we can deal with. But only someone who is ready for everything, who doesn't exclude any experience, even the most incomprehensible, will live the relationship with another person as something alive and will himself sound the depths of his own being. For if we imagine this being of the individual as a larger or smaller room, it is obvious that most people come to know only one corner of their room, one spot near the window, one narrow strip on which they keep walking back and forth. In this way they have a certain security. And yet how much more human is the dangerous in security that drives those prisoners in Poe's stories to feel out the shapes of their horrible dungeons and not be strangers to the unspeakable terror of their cells. We, however, are not prisoners. No traps or snares have been set around us, and there is nothing that should frighten or upset us. We have been put into life as into the element we most accord with, and we have, moreover, through thousands of years of adaptation, come to resemble this life so greatly that when we hold still, through a fortunate mimicry we can hardly be differentiated from everything around us. We have no reason to harbor any mistrust against our world, for it is not against us. If it has terrors, they are our terrors; if it has abysses, these abysses belong to us; if there are dangers, we must try to love them. And if only we arrange our life in accordance with the principle which tells us that we must always trust in the difficult, then what now appears to us as the most alien will become our most intimate and trusted experience. How could we forget those ancient myths that stand at the beginning of all races, the myths about dragons that at the last moment are transformed into princesses? Perhaps all the dragons in our lives are princesses who are only waiting to see us act, just once, with beauty and courage. Perhaps everything that frightens us is, in its deepest essence, something helpless that wants our love.

So you mustn't be frightened, dear Mr. Kappus, if a sadness rises in front of you, larger than any you have ever seen; if an anxiety, like light and cloud-shadows, moves over your hands and over everything you do. You must realize that something is happening to you, that life has not forgotten you, that it holds you in its hand and will not let you fall. Why do you want to shut out of your life any uneasiness, any misery, any depression, since after all you don't know what work these conditions are doing inside you? Why do you want to persecute yourself with the question of where all this is coming from and where it is going? Since you know, after all, that you are in the midst of transitions and you wished for nothing so much as to change. If there is anything unhealthy in your reactions, just bear in mind that sickness is the means by which an organism frees itself from what is alien; so one must simply help it to be sick, to have its whole sickness and to break out with it, since that is the way it gets better. In you, dear Mr. Kappus, so much is happening now; you must be patient like someone who is sick, and confident like someone who is recovering; for perhaps you are both. And more: you are also the doctor, who has to watch over himself. But in every sickness there are many days when the doctor can do nothing but wait. And that is what you, insofar as you are your own doctor, must now do, more than anything else.

Don't observe yourself too closely. Don't be too quick to draw conclusions from what happens to you; simply let it happen. Otherwise it will be too easy for you to look with blame (that is: morally) at your past, which naturally has a share in everything that now meets you. But whatever errors, wishes, and yearnings of your boyhood are operating in you now are not what you remember and condemn. The extraordinary circumstances of a solitary and helpless childhood are so difficult, so complicated, surrendered to so many influences and at the same time so cut off from all real connection with life that, where a vice enters it, one may not simply call it a vice. One must be so careful with names anyway; it is so often the name of an offense that a life shatters upon, not the nameless and personal action itself, which was perhaps a quite definite necessity of that life and could have been absorbed by it without any trouble. And the expenditure of energy seems to you so great only because you overvalue victory; it is not the "great thing" that you think you have achieved, although you are right about your feeling; the great thing is that there was already something there which you could replace that deception with, something true and real. Without this even your victory would have been just a moral reaction of no great significance; but in fact it has become a part of your life. Your life, dear Mr. Kappus, which I think of with so many good wishes. Do you remember how that life yearned out of childhood toward the "great thing"? I see that it is now yearning forth beyond the great thing toward the greater one. That is why it does not cease to be difficult, but that is also why it will not cease to grow.

And if there is one more thing that I must say to you, it is this: Don't think that the person who is trying to comfort you now lives untroubled among the simple and quiet words that sometimes give you pleasure. His life has much trouble and sadness, and remains far behind yours. If it were otherwise, he would never have been able to find those words.

Yours,
Rainer Maria Rilke

Letter Nine

Furuborg, Jonsered, in Sweden
November 4, 1904

My dear Mr. Kappus,

During this time that has passed without a letter, I have been partly traveling, partly so busy that I couldn't write. And even today writing is difficult for me, because I have already had to write so many letters that my hand is tired. If I could dictate, I would have much more to say to you, but as it is, please accept these few words as an answer to your long letter.

I think of you often, dear Mr. Kappus, and with such concentrated good wishes that somehow they ought to help you. Whether my letters really are a help, I often doubt. Don't say, "Yes, they are." Just accept them calmly and without many thanks, and let us wait for what wants to come.

There is probably no point in my going into your questions now; for what I could say about your tendency to doubt or about your inability to bring your outer and inner lives into harmony or about all the other things that oppress you-: is just what I have already said: just the wish that you may find in yourself enough patience to endure and enough simplicity to have faith; that you may gain more and more confidence in what is difficult and in your solitude among other people. And as for the rest, let life happen to you. Believe me: life is in the right, always.

And about feelings: All feelings that concentrate you and lift you up are pure; only that feeling is impure which grasps just one side of your being and thus distorts you. Everything you can think of as you face your childhood, is good. Everything that makes more of you than you have ever been, even in your best hours, is right. Every intensification is good, if it is in your entire blood, if it isn't intoxication or muddiness, but joy which you can see into, clear to the bottom. Do you understand what I mean?

And your doubt can become a good quality if you train it. It must become knowing, it must become criticism. Ask it, whenever it wants to spoil something for you, why something is ugly, demand proofs from it, test it, and you will find it perhaps bewildered and embarrassed, perhaps also protesting. But don't give in, insist on arguments, and act in this way, attentive and persistent, every single time, and the day will come when, instead of being a destroyer, it will become one of your best workers - perhaps the most intelligent of all the ones that are building your life.

That is all, dear Mr. Kappus, that I am able to tell you today. But I am sending you, along with this letter, the reprint of a small poem[2] that has just appeared in the Prague German Labor. In it I speak to you further of life and death and of how both are great and glorious.

Yours,
Rainer Maria Rilke

---

[2] 'The Lay of Love and Death of Cornet Christoph Rilke,' written in 1899 and first published in book form in 1906.

This brief novel about a young soldier in the Austro-Turkish war of the early 1660's was written during a single night in 1899, when Rilke was twenty-three. It had a modest success when it first came out. But when it was republished in 1912, in a more popular format, it took Germany by storm, much to the author's amazement. The first edition was sold out within weeks; there was one new printing after another; soldiers on the front lines during the World War I carried the book in their knapsacks, along with, possibly, the Bible. By 1920 it had sold 200,000 copies – an astounding figure for that time – and by the late '50's over a million. An intensely romantic meditation on the nature of masculinity, it is the book by which, among German readers, Rilke was primarily known and loved.

Letter Ten

Paris
The day after Christmas, 1908

You must know, dear Mr. Kappus, how glad I was to have the lovely letter from you. The news that you give me, real and expressible as it now is again, seems to me good news, and the longer I thought it over, the more I felt that it was very good news indeed. That is really what I wanted to write you for Christmas Eve; but I have been variously and uninterruptedly living in my work this winter, and the ancient holiday arrived so quickly that I hardly had enough time to do the most necessary errands, much less to write.

But I have thought of you often during this holiday and imagined how silent you must be in your solitary fort among the empty hills, upon which those large southern winds fling themselves as if they wanted to devour them in large pieces.

It must be immense, this silence, in which sounds and movements have room, and if one thinks that along with all this the presence of the distant sea also resounds, perhaps as the innermost note in this prehistoric harmony, then one can only wish that you are trustingly and patiently letting the magnificent solitude work upon you, this solitude which can no longer be erased from your life; which, in everything that is in store for you to experience and to do, will act an anonymous influence, continuously and gently decisive, rather as the blood of our ancestors incessantly moves in us and combines with our own to form the unique, unrepeatable being that we are at every turning of our life.

Yes: I am glad you have that firm, sayable existence with you, that title, that uniform, that service, all that tangible and limited world, which in such surroundings, with such an isolated and not numerous body of men, takes on seriousness and necessity, and implies a vigilant application, above and beyond the frivolity and mere time passing of the military profession, and not only permits a self-reliant attentiveness but actually cultivates it. And to be in circumstances that are working upon us, that from time to time place us in front of great natural Things - that is all we need.

Art too is just a way of living, and however one lives, one can, without knowing, prepare for it; in everything real one is closer to it, more its neighbor, than in the unreal half-artistic professions, which, while they pretend to be close to art, in practice deny and attack the existence of all art - as, for example, all of journalism does and almost all criticism and three quarters of what is called (and wants to be called) literature. I am glad, in a word, that you have overcome the danger of landing in one of those professions, and are solitary and courageous, somewhere in a rugged reality. May the coming year support and strengthen you in that.

Always
Yours, R. M. Rilke

Kings in Legends[3]

Kings in old legends seem
Like mountains rising in the evening light.
They blind all with their gleam,
Their loins encircled are by girdles bright,
Their robes are edged with bands
Of precious stones — the rarest earth affords —
With richly jeweled hands
They hold their slender, shining, naked swords.

Rainer Maria Rilke, 1875-1926
From *The Book of Pictures*

[3] In *The Book of Pictures,* Rilke's art reaches its culmination on what might be termed its monumental side. The visualization is elevated to the impersonal objective level which gives to the rhythm of these poems an imperturbable calm, to the figures presented a monumental erectness. *The Men of the House of Colonna, The Czars, Charles XII Riding Through the Ukraine* are portrayed each with his individual historical gesture, with a luminosity as strong as the color and movement which they gave to their time. In the mythical poem, *Kings in Legends,* this concrete element in the art of Rilke has found perhaps its supreme expression -

The Knight

The Knight rides forth in coat of mail
Into the roar of the world.
And here is Life: the vines in the vale
And friend and foe, and the feast in the hall,
And May and the maid, and the glen and the grail;
God's flags afloat on every wall
In a thousand streets unfurled.

Beneath the armour of the Knight
Behind the chain's black links
Death crouches and thinks and thinks:
"When will the sword's blade sharp and bright
Forth from the scabbard spring
And cut the network of the cloak
Enmeshing me ring on ring—
When will the foe's delivering stroke
Set me free
To dance
And sing?"

The Woman Who Loves

Ah yes! I long for you. To you I glide
And lose myself—for to you I belong.
The hope that hitherto I have denied
Imperious comes to me as from your side
Serious, unfaltering and swift and strong.

Those times: the times when I was quite alone
By memories wrapt that whispered to me low,
My silence was the quiet of a stone
Over which rippling murmuring waters flow.

But in these weeks of the awakening Spring
Something within me has been freed—something
That in the past dark years unconscious lay,
Which rises now within me and commands
And gives my poor warm life into your hands
Who know not what I was that Yesterday.